Preface

Oracle Certified Associate Java Programmer OCAJP 1Z0 808 certification represents a significant milestone for individuals seeking to establish a strong foundation in the world of Java programming. It serves as a testament to their commitment to excellence, their dedication to mastering the essential concepts of Java, and their determination to embark on a fulfilling and rewarding career in the field of software development. This book, "Oracle Certified Associate Java Programmer: A Comprehensive Guide," is a culmination of the collective wisdom, practical insights, and industry expertise of seasoned professionals and educators who have meticulously curated a comprehensive learning resource designed to guide and empower OCAJP aspirants on their journey to achieving this esteemed certification.

Understanding the multifaceted nature of the OCAJP examination, this book takes a comprehensive approach that goes beyond the mere assimilation of theoretical knowledge. It delves into the intricacies of Java programming, covering foundational topics such as data types, control structures, arrays, and methods, while also exploring more advanced concepts such as inheritance, polymorphism, and exception handling. By providing a balanced blend of theoretical explanations, practical examples, and hands-on exercises, this book aims to foster a deep and intuitive understanding of Java's core principles, enabling readers to develop the analytical and problem-solving skills necessary to excel in the OCAJP examination and, more importantly, in real-world programming scenarios.

Moreover, this book emphasizes the significance of practical application and critical thinking, encouraging readers to not only grasp the theoretical concepts but also to apply them to practical situations. By presenting coding exercises, case studies, and real-world scenarios, it seeks to cultivate a holistic learning experience that instills confidence, creativity, and a thorough understanding of best practices in Java programming. By illuminating the underlying principles and industry-relevant techniques, this book aims to equip OCAJP aspirants with the knowledge and skill set necessary to navigate the complexities of the certification examination and to lay a solid foundation for their future endeavors in the ever-evolving landscape of Java programming.

Table of Contents

Chapter 1 : The Oracle Certified Associate Java Programmer Part 1

1. Which of the following is a valid JavaBean method signature?

A. public void getArrow()

B. public void setBow()

C. public void setRange(int range)

D. public String addTarget(String target)

Answer: C

2. Given the code fragment:

```
int a = 3;
int b = 2;
int c = 1;
int r1 = a * b / c + 1;
int r2 = a / b * c + 1;
int r3 = a * (b / (c + 1));
System.out.println(r1 + " : " + r2 + " : " + r3);
```

What is the result?

A. 2 : 7 : 3
B. 7 : 7 : 9
C. 2 : 7 : 0
D. 7 : 2 : 3

Answer: D

3. Given:

```
public class Test {

    public static void main(String[] args) {
        if (args[0].equals("Hello") ? true : false) {
            System.out.println("Success");
        } else {
            System.out.println("Failure");
        }
    }
}
```

And given the commands:

```
javac Test.java
Java Test Hello
```

What is the result?

A. Success

B. Failure

C. Compilation fails

D. An exception is thrown at runtime

Answer: A

4. Which statement is true about the default constructor of a top-level class?

A. It can take arguments.

B. It has private access modifier in its declaration.

C. It can be overloaded.

D. The default constructor of a subclass always invokes the no-argument constructor of its
superclass.

Answer: D

5. Bytecode is in a file with which extension?

A. bytecode

B. .bytes

C..class

D..exe

E. .javac

F. .Java

Answer. C

6. Given the code fragment:

```
int a[] = {1, 2, 3, 4, 5};
for(XXX) {
    System.out.print(a[e]);
}
```

Which option can replace xxx to enable the code to print 135?

A. int e = 0; e < = 4; e++

B. int e=0;e<5;e +=2

C. int e = 1; e<=5; e+=1

D. int e=1; e<5; e+=2

Answer: B

7. Given the code fragment:

```
public static void main(String[] args) {
    boolean opt = true;
    switch (opt) {
        case true:
            System.out.print("True");
            break;
        default:
            System.out.print("***");
    }
    System.out.println("Done");
}
```

Which modification enables the code fragment to print TrueDone?

A. Replace line 5 With String opt = "true"; Replace line 7 with case "true".

B. Replace line 5 with boolean opt= 1; Replace line 7 with case 1:

C. At line 9, remove the break statement.

D. Remove the default section.

Answer: A

8. Which of the following are checked exceptions? (Choose all that apply)

A. Exception

B.IllegalArgumentException

C. IOException

D. NullPointerException

E. NumberFormatException

F. StackOverf10wError

Answer: A, C.

9. Of the following four modifiers, choose the one that is not implicitly applied to all interface variables.

A. final

B. abstract

C. static

D. public

Answer: B

10. Given the code fragment:

```
int a = 3;
int b = 2;
int c = 1;
int r1 = a * b / c + 1;
int r2 = a / b * c + 1;
int r3 = a * (b / (c + 1));
System.out.println(r1 + " : " + r2 + " : " + r3);
```

What is the result?

A. 2 : 7 : 3

B. 7 : 7 : 9

C. 2 : 7 : 0

D. 7 : 2 : 3

Answer: D

11. Given:

```
public class MyClass {
public static void main(String[] args) {
while (int ii = 0; ii < 2) {
ii++;
System.out.println("ii = " + ii);
}
}
}
```

What is the result?

A. ii = 1 ii = 2

B. Compilation fails

C. The program prints nothing

D. The program goes into an infinite loop with no output

E. The program goes to an infinite loop outputting: ii = 1 ii = 1

Answer: B

12. Which three are advantages of the Java exception mechanism?

A. Provides a set of standard exceptions that covers all possible errors

B. Allows the creation of new exceptions that are customized to the particular program being created

C. Improves the program structure because exceptions must be handled in the method in which they occurre

D. Improves the program structure because the programmer can choose where to handle exceptions

E. Improves the program structure because the error handling code is separated from the normal program function

Answer: B,D,E

13. Given:

```
public class MarkList {
int num;
public static void graceMarks(MarkList obj4) {
obj4.num += 10;
}
public static void main(String[] args) {
MarkList obj1 = new MarkList();
MarkList obj2 = obj1;
MarkList obj3 = new MarkList();
obj2.num = 60;
graceMarks(obj2);
}
}
```

How many objects are created in the memory runtime?

A. 1

B. 2

C. 3

D. 4

Answer: B

14. Restricting access to only the public methods of a class is related to which one of these concepts in Java?

A. Platform independence

B. Object orientation

C. Encapsulation

D. Inheritance

Answer: C

15. Given the code fragment:

```
int x = 10;
int y = ++x;
int z = 0;
if (y >= 10 | y <= ++x) {
    z = x;
} else {
    z = x++;
}
System.out.println(z);
```

What is the result?

A. 11

B. 10

C. 12

D. A compile time error occurs.

Answer: C

16. "You have a list orders of PurchaseOrder objects, each with a date, a Customer and a state. You want filter list in various ways"

Which of the following in built functional interface you are going to use for above?

A. UnaryOperator<T>

B. Consumer<T>

C. Supplier<T>

D. Predicate<T>

Answer: D

17. Given the classes:

* AssertionError

* ArithmeticException

* ArrayIndexOutOfBoundsException

* FileNotFoundException

* IllegalArgumentException

* IOError

* IOException

* NumberFormatException

* SQLException

Which option lists only those classes that belong to the unchecked exception category?

A. ArrayIndexOutOfBoundsException, ArithmeticException

B. AssertionError, IOError, IOException

C. ArithmeticException, FileNotFoundException, NumberFormatException

D. FileNotFoundException, IOException, SQLException

E. ArrayIndexOutOfBoundException, IllegalArgumentException, FileNotFoundException

Answer: A

18. Given the code fragment:

```
char colorCode = 'y';
switch (colorCode) {
  case 'r':
       int color = 100;
       break;
  case 'b':
       color = 10;
       break;
  case 'y':
       color = 1;
       break;
 }
 System.out.println(color);
```

What is the result?

A. It results in a compile time error at line 18.

B. It results in a compile time error at line 9.

C. It prints : 1

D. It results in a compile time error at lines at lines 12 and 15.

Answer: A

19.Which of the following print out a date representing April 1, 2015? (Choose all that apply)a

A. `System.out.println(LocalDate.of(2015, Calendar.APRIL, 1));`

B. `System.out.println(LocalDate.of(2015, Month.APRIL, 1));`

C. `System.out.println(LocalDate.of(2015, 3, 1));`

D. `System.out.println(LocalDate.of(2015, 4, 1));`

E. `System.out.println(new LocalDate(2015, 3, 1));`

Answer. B, D.

20. Given: Acc.java:

```
package p1;
public class Acc {
    int p;
    private int q;
    protected int r;
    public int s;
}
```

Test.java:

```
package p2;
import p1.Acc;
public class Test extends Acc {
    public static void main(String[] args) {
        Acc obj = new Test();
    }
}
```

Which statement is true?

A.Both p and s are accessible via obj.

B. Only s is accessible via obj.

C. Both r and s are accessible via obj.

D. p, r, and s are accessible via obj.

Answer: B

21. Given:

```
abstract class X {
public abstract void methodX();
}
interface Y{
public void methodY();
}
```

Which two code fragments are valid?

A) class Z extends X implements Y {
public void methodZ(){}
}

B) abstract class Z extends X implements Y {
public void methodZ(){}
}

C) class Z extends X implements Y {
public void methodX(){}
public void methodY(){}
}

D) abstract class Z extends X implements Y {
}

E) class Z extends X implements Y {
public void methodY(){}
}

A. Option A

B. Option B

C. Option C

D. Option D

E. Option E

Answer: B, C, D

22. Given the class definitions:

```
class C1 {}
class C2 extends C1 {}
class C3 extends C2 {}
```

and the code fragment:

```
C1 obj1 = (C1) new C2();
C2 obj2 = (C2) new C3();
C2 obj3 = (C2) new C1();
C3 obj4 = (C3) obj2;
```

Which line throws ClassCastException?

A. line 18

B. line 17

C. line 19

D. line 16

Answer: D

23.What is the value of that Number after the execution of the following code snippet?

```
long thatNumber = 5 >= 5 ? 1+2 : 1*1;
if(++thatNumber < 4)     thatNumber += 1;
```

A. 3

B. 4

C. 5

D. The Answer cannot be determined until runtime.

Answer: B

24. Which of the following data types will allow the following code snippet to compile?

```
float i=4;
float j=2;
____z=i+j;
```

A. long

B. double

C. int

D. float

E. byte

Answer: B, D

25. What individual changes, if any, would allow the following code to compile?

(Choose all that apply)

```
1: public interface Animal { public default String getName()
{ return null; } }
2: interface Mammal { public default String getName() {
return null; } }
3: abstract class Otter implements Mammal, Animal {}
```

A. The code compiles without issue.

B. Remove the default method modifier and methodimplementation on line 1.

C. Remove the default method modifier and methodimplementation on line 2.

D. Remove the default method modifier and methodimplementation on lines 1 and 2.

E. Change the return value on line 1 from null to "Animal".

G. Override the getName() method with an abstract method inthe Otter class.

H. Override the getName( ) method with a concrete method inthe Otter class.

Answer. D, F, G.

26. Which usage represents a valid way of compiling java source file with the name "Main"?

A. javac Main.java

B. java Main.class

C. java Main.java

D. javac Main

E. java Main

Answer: A

27. Which two features can be implemented in a Java application by encapsulating the entity classes used? (Choose two.)

A. data validation

B. compile time polymorphism

C. data hiding

D. data abstraction

E. data memory optimization

Answer: C,D

28. Assuming we have a valid, non-null HenHouse object whose value is initialized by the blank line shown here, which of the following are possible outputs of this application?

(Choose all that apply)

```
1: class Chicken {}
2: interface HenHouse { public java.util.List<Chicken>
getChickens(); }
3: public class ChickenSong {
4:   public static void main(String[] args) {
5:     HenHouse house = ____________
6:     Chicken chicken = house.getChickens().get(0);
7:     for(int i=0; i<house.getChickens().size();
8:       chicken = house.getChickens().get(i++)) {
9:       System.out.println("Cluck");
10: } } }
```

A.The code will not compile because of line 6.

B. The code will not compile because of lines 7—8.

C. The application will compile but not produce any output.

D. The application will output Cluck exactly once.

E. The application will output Cluck more than once.

F. The application will compile but produce an exception atruntime.

Answer. D, E, F.

29. If a try statement has catch blocks for both Exception and IOException, then which of the following statements is correct?

A. The catch block for Exception must appear before the catch block for IOException.

B. The catch block for IOException must appear before the catch block for Exception.

C. The catch blocks for these two exception types can be declared in any order.

D. A try statement cannot be declared with these two catch block types because they are incompatible.

Answer: B

30. Which of the following lines can be inserted at line 11 to print true? (Choose all that apply)

```
10: public static void main(String[] args) {
11:   // INSERT CODE HERE
12: }
13: private static boolean test(Predicate<Integer> p) {
14:   return p.test(5);
15: }
```

A. System.out.println(test(i -> i = =5));

B. System.out.println(test(i -> {i = = 5;}));

C. System.out.println(test(i) -> {i = = 5));

D. System.out.println(test((**int** i)-> i = = 5);

E. System.out.println(test((**int** i) -> {**return** i = = 5;}));

F. System.out.println(test(i)-> {return i = = 5;}));

Answer- A, C, F.

31. Given the code fragment:

```
int nums1[] = {1, 2, 3};
int nums2[] = {1, 2, 3, 4, 5};
nums 2 = nums 1;
for (int x : nums2){
    System.out.print(x + ":");
}
```

What is the result?

A. 1:2:3:4:5:

B. 1:2:3:

C. Compilation fails.

D. An ArrayOutOfBoundsException is thrown at runtime

Answer: B

32. Given the following class declarations:

public abstract class Animal

public interface Hunter

public class Cat extends Animal implements Hunter

public class Tiger extends Cat

Which Answer fails to compile?

```
A) ArrayList<Animal> myList = new ArrayList<>();
   myList.add(new Tiger());

B) ArrayList<Hunter> myList = new ArrayList<>();
   myList.add(new Cat());

C) ArrayList<Hunter> myList = new ArrayList<>();
   myList.add(new Tiger());

D) ArrayList<Tiger> myList = new ArrayList<>();
   myList.add(new Cat());

E) ArrayList<Animal> myList = new ArrayLIst<>();
   myList.add(new Cat());
```

A.Option A

B. Option B

C. Option C

D. Option D

E. Option E

Answer: E

33. Which of the following statements can be inserted in the blank line so that the code will compile successfully? (Choose all that apply)

```
public interface CanSwim {}
public class Amphibian implements CanSwim {}
class Tadpole extends Amphibian {}

public class FindAllTadPole {
  public static void main(String[] args) {
    List<Tadpole> tadpoles = new ArrayList<Tadpole>();
    for(Amphibian amphibian : tadpoles) {
      __________ tadpole = amphibian;
} } }
```

A. CanSwim

B. Long

C. Amphibian

D. Tadpole

E. Object

Answer. A, C, E.

34. What is the result of the following program?

```
public class Egret {
  private String color;
  public Egret() {
    this("white");
  }
  public Egret(String color) {
    color = color;
  }

 public static void main(String[] args) {
   Egret e = new Egret();
   System.out.println("Color:" + e.color);
  }
}
```

A. Color:

B. Color: null

C. Color:White

D. Compiler error on line 4.

E. Compiler error on line 10

F. Compiler error on line 11.

Answer B

35. You are writing a method that is declared not to return a value. Which two are permitted in the method body?

A. omission of the return statement

B. return null;

C. return void;

D. return;

Answer: A,D

36. Given the code fragment:

```
public static void main(String[] args) {
    int iVar = 100;
    float fVar = 100.100f;
    double dVar = 123;
    fVar = iVar;
    iVar = fVar;
    fVar = dVar;
    dVar = fVar;
    iVar = dVar;
    dVar = iVar;
}
```

Which three lines fail to compile? (Choose three.)

A. Line 7

B. Line 8

C. Line 9

D. Line 10

E. Line 11

F. Line 12

Answer: A, D, F

37. Given:

```
class Product {
    int id;
    String name;
    Product (int id, String name) {
        this.id = id;
        this.name = name;
    }
}
public class Shop {
    public static void main(String[] args) {
        List<Product> 1st = new ArrayList<>();
        1st.add(new Product(10, "IceCream"));
        1st.add(new Product(11, "Chocolate"));
        Product p1 = new Product(10, "IceCream");
        System.out.println(1st.indexOf(p1));
    }
}
```

What is the result?

A. true

B. false

C. -1

D. 0

Answer: C

38. What is the output of the following program?

```
1: public class BearOrShark {

    public static void main(String[] args) {
      int luck = 10;
      if((luck>10 ? luck++: --luck)<10) {
        System.out.print("Bear");
      } if(luck<10) System.out.print("Shark");
  } }
```

A. Bear

B.Shark

C. BearShark

D. The code will not compile because of line 4.

E. The code will not compile because of line 6.

F. The code compiles without issue but does not produce anyoutput.

Answer : C

39. Given:

```
interface Readable {
    public void readBook();
    public void setBookMark();
}

abstract class Book implements Readable {    // line n1
    public void readBook() { }
    // line n2
}

class EBook extends Book {                   // line n3
    public void readBook() { }
    // line n4
}
```

And given the code fragment:

Book book1 = new EBook();

book1.readBook();

Which option enables the code to compile?

A) Replace the code fragment at `line n1` with:
`class Book implements Readable {`

B) At `line n2` insert:
`public abstract void setBookMark();`

C) Replace the code fragment at `line n3` with:
`abstract class EBook extends Book {`

D) At `line n4` insert:
`public void setBookMark() { }`

A. Option A

B. Option B

C. Option C

D. Option D

Answer: D

40. Given the code fragment:

```
public static void main(String[] args) {
    String str = " ";
    str.trim();
    System.out.println(str.equals("") + " " + str.isEmpty());
}
```

What is the result?

A. true true

B. true false

C. false false

D. false true

Answer: C

41. Given:

```
public class Test {
    public static void main(String[] args) {
        Test ts = new Test();
        System.out.print(isAvailable + " ");
        isAvailable= ts.doStuff();
        System.out.println(isAvailable);
    }
    public static boolean doStuff() {
        return !isAvailable;
    }
    static boolean isAvailable = true;
}
```

What is the result?

A. Compilation fails.

B. false true

C. true false

D. true true

E. false false

Answer: C

42. Which statement best describes encapsulation?

A. Encapsulation ensures that classes can be designed so that if a method has an argument MyType x, any subclass of MyType can be passed to that method.

B. Encapsulation ensures that classes can be designed so that only certain fields and methods of an object are accessible from other objects.

C. Encapsulation ensures that classes can be designed so that their methods are inheritable.

D. Encapsulation ensures that classes can be designed with some fields and methods declared as abstract.

Answer: B

43. Given:

```
public class App {
     int foo;
     static int bar;

     static void process() {
          foo += 10;
          bar += 10;
     }
     public static void main(String[] args) {
          App firstObj = new App();
          App.process();
          System.out.println(firstObj.bar);

          App secondObj = new App();
          App.process();
          System.out.println(secondObj.bar);
     }
}
```

What is the result?

A. 10
20

B. A compile time error occurs

C. 20
20

D. 10
10

Answer: B

44. Which three statements describe the object-oriented features of the Java language?

(Choose three.)

A. Objects can be reused.

B. A subclass must override the methods from a superclass.

C. Objects can share behaviors with other objects.

D. A package must contain a main class.

E. Object is the root class of all other objects.

F. A main method must be declared in every class.

Answer: B,C,F

45. Given the code fragment:

```
char colorCode = 'y';
switch (colorCode) {
  case 'r':
       int color = 100;
       break;
  case 'b':
       color = 10;
       break;
  case 'y':
       color = 1;
       break;
 }
 System.out.println(color);
```

What is the result?

A. It results in a compile time error at line 18.

B. It results in a compile time error at line 9.

C. It prints : 1

D. It results in a compile time error at lines at lines 12 and 15.

Answer: A

46. Given:

```
public static void main(String[] args) {
    String ta = "A ";
    ta = ta.concat("B ");
    String tb = "C ";
    ta = ta.concat(tb);
    ta.replace('C', 'D');
    ta = ta.concat(tb);
    System.out.println(ta);
}
```

What is the result?

A. A B C D

B. A C D

C. A C D D

D. A B D

E. A B D C

Answer: C

47. Given the code fragment:

```
StringBuilder sb1 = new StringBuilder("Duke");
String str1 = sb1.toString();
// insert code here
  System.out.print(str1 == str2);
```

Which code fragment, when inserted at line 9, enables the code to print true?

A. String str2 = str1;

B. String str2 = new String(str1);

C. String str2 = sb1. toString();

D. String str2 = "Duke";

Answer: A

48. Given

```
class Test{

    public static void main(String[] args){
     int []a = {1,2,3,4,5,6};
     int i = a.length;.
          while(i>=1){
               System.out.print(a[i]);
              i–;
          }
     }
}
```

What would be the output, if it is executed as a program?

A. 123456

B. 65432

C. 12345

D. An exception could be thrown at runtime.

E. Compile error.

Answer: D

49. Given

```
class Ex6{
        public static void main(String args[]){
                int i = 0, j=10;
                try{
                        j /=i;
                }
                System.out.print("Divide by Zero!");
                catch(Exception e){
                        System.out.print("error");
                 }
        }
}
```

What is the output?

A. 0

B. 0 Divide by Zero!

C. Divide by Zero! Error

D. Error

E. Compilation fails.

F. An uncaught exception is thrown at runtime.

Answer: D

50. Consider

A and E are Classes

B and D are interfaces

C is an abstract class

Which are true? (Choose 3)

A. class F implements B ,C{ }

B. class F implements B{ }

C. class F extends A,E{ }

D. class F extends E{ }

E. class F implements B,D{ }

Answer: A, B, E

51. Given the code fragment:

```
public static void main(String[] args) {
    int ii = 0;
    int jj = 7;
    for (ii = 0; ii < jj - 1; ii = ii + 2) {
        System.out.print(ii + " ");
    }
}
```

What is the result?

A. 2 4

B. 0 2 4 6

C. 0 2 4

D. Compilation fails

Answer: C

52. Given

```
class Test{
    public static void main(String[] args) {
        int a[] = {};
        System.out.print(a instanceof Object);
    }
}
```

Note: The keyword "instanceof" is use to check whether an object is of a particular type

Which is true?

A. Will produce output as false.

B. Compilation fails due to error at line 3.

C. Will produce output as true.

D. Compilation fails due to error at line 4.

E. Length of this array is 3.

Answer: C

53. Given the code fragment:

```
public static void main(String[] args) {
    StringBuilder sb = new StringBuilder("Java");
    String s = "Java" ;

    if (sb.toString().equals(s.toString())) {
        System.out.println("Match 1");
    } else if (sb.equals(s)) {
        System.out.println("Match 2");
    } else {
        System.out.println("No Match");
    }
}
```

What is the result?

A. Match 1

B. Match 2

C. No Match

D. A NullPointerException is thrown at runtime.

Answer: A

54. Given

```
class Program{

    static Integer i;

    public static void main(String [] args){
        try{
            System.out.println(i.compareTo(0));
        }catch ( ArithmeticException | NullPointerException e){
            System.out.println("Exception");
        }
    }
}
```

Which is the output?

A. -1

B. 0

C. 1

D. Exception

E. Compilation fails.

Answer: D

55. Examine the content of App.java

```
package p1;
public class App {
    public static void main(String[] args) {
        System.out.println("Java");
    }
}
```

and of `Test.java`:

```
package p1.p2;
public class Test {}
```

Which is true?

A. The App.class file is stored within the p1 folder. The Test.class file is stored within the p2 sub-folder of p1.

B. The App class is accessible within the Test class without an import statement.

C. import p1.App; is used to access the App class within the Test class.

D. It is optional to have the package statement as the first line of class definitions.

Answer:C

56.Given

```
class Ex1{
    public static void main(String[] args) {
        int a[] = { 1,2,053,4};
        int b[][] = { {1,2,4} , {2,2,1},{0,43,2}};
        System.out.print(a[3]==b[0][2] );
        System.out.print(" " + (a[2]==b[2][1]));
    }
}
```

Which is the output?

A. true false

B. false false

C. false true

D. true true

E. Compilation fails

Answer: D

57. Choose three legal identifiers.

A. 2ndtName

B. _8_

C.&name

D. $

E. new

Answer: B,D,E

58. Given:

```
public class FieldInit {
    Character c;
    boolean b;
    float f;
    void printAll() {
        System.out.println("c = " + c);
        System.out.println("b = " + b);
        System.out.println("f = " + f);
    }

    public static void main(String[] args) {
        FieldInit f = new FieldInit();
        f.printAll();
    }
}
```

What is the result?

A. c=null
b=true f=0.0

B. c=
b=false
f=0.0

C. c=null
b=false
f=0.0

D. c=0
b=false
f=0.0F

Answer:C

59. Given the code fragment

```
public class Test {
    public static void main(String[] args) {
        /* insert code here */
        array[0]=10;
        array[1]=20;
        System.out.print(array[0]+":"+array[1]);
    }
}
```

Which code fragment, when inserted at line 3, enables the code to print 10:20?

A. `int[] array  = new int[1];`

B. `int[] array;`
`array = new int[2];`

C. `int array = new int[2];`

D. `int array[1];`

Answer: B

60. Given

```
class Test{
        int value = 10;
        public static void main(String[] args) {
                new Test ().print();
        }
        public void print(){
                int value = 8;
                System.out.print(value);
        }
}
```

Which is the output?

A. 8

B. 10.

C. Compilation fails due to error at line 4.

D. Compilation fails due to error at line 7.

Answer: A

61. Given the code fragment:

```
public static void main(String[] args) {
    try {
        int num = 10;
        int div = 0;
        int ans = nim / div;
    } catch (ArithmeticExeption ae) {
        ans = 0                                    // line n1
    } catch (Exception e) {
        System.out.println("Invalid calculation");
    }
    System.out.println("Answer = " + ans);     // line n2
}
```

What is the result?

A. Answer = 0

B. Invalid calculation

C. Compilation fails only at line n1.

D. Compilation fails only at line n2.

E. Compilation fails at line n1 and line2.

Answer: E

62. Given:

[illegible]

What is the result?

A. myStr: 9009, myNum: 9009

B. myStr: 7007, myNum: 7007

C. myStr: 7007, myNum: 9009

D. Compilation fails

Answer: C

63. Given

```
class Test{
    static int x = 0;
    public static void main(String[] args) {
        for(int x=0;x<5;x++){    }
        System.out.print(x);
}}
```

Which is the output?

A. 4

B. 5

C. 0

D. Compilation fails.

E. Runtime exception will be thrown.

Answer: C

64. Given

```
class Exer{
    public static void main(String [] args){
        String s = “Java”;
        s.concat(” SE 7″);
        s.replaceAll(“7″,””);
        System.out.print(s);
}}
```

What is the result?

A. Java SE “”

B. Java SE 7

C. Java SE

D. Java.

E. Compilation fails.

Answer:D

65. Given the code fragment:

```
public static void main(String[] args) {
    int ii = 0;
    int jj = 7;
    for (ii = 0; ii < jj - 1; ii = ii + 2) {
        System.out.print(ii + " ");
    }
}
```

What is the result?

A. 2 4

B. 0 2 4 6

C. 0 2 4

D. Compilation fails

Answer: C

66.Given the code fragment:

```
int nums1[] = {1, 2, 3};
int nums2[] = {1, 2, 3, 4, 5};
nums 2 = nums 1;
for (int x : nums2){
    System.out.print(x + ":");
}
```

What is the result?

A. 1:2:3:4:5:
B. 1:2:3:
C. Compilation fails.
D. An `ArrayOutOfBoundsException` is thrown at runtime.

Answer: B

67. Given the code fragment:

```
class X {
    public void printFileContent() {
        /* code goes here */
        throw new IOException();
    }
}
public class Test {
    public static void main(String[] args) {
        X xobj = new X();
        xobj.printFileContent();
    }
}
```

Which two modifications should you make so that the code compiles successfully? (Choose two.)

☐ A) Replace line 8 with `public static void main(String[] args) throws Exception {`

☐ B) Replace line 10 with:
```
try {
    xobj.printFileContent();
}
catch(Exception e) { }
catch(IOException e) { }
```

☐ C) Replace line 2 with `public void printFileContent() throws IOException {`

☐ D) Replace line 4 with `throw IOException("Exception raised");`

☐ E) At line 11, insert `throw new IOException();`

A. Option A
B. Option B
C. Option C
D. Option D
E. Option E
Answer: A,C

68. Given:

```
class Caller {
    private void init () {
        System.out.println("Initialized");
    }

    private void start () {
    init();
    System.out.println("Started");
    }
}

public class TestCall {
    public static void main(String[] args) {
        Caller c = new Caller();
        c.start(); // line n1
        c.init();  // line n2
    }
}
```

What is the result?
A. Compilation fails at line n1.
B. Initialized Started Initialized
C. Initialized Started
D. Compilation fails at line n2.
Answer: A

69. Given the following segment of code

```
ArrayList<Vehicle> myList = new ArrayList<>();
myList.add(new Motorcycle());
```

Which two statements, if either were true, would make the code compile?

A. Vehicle is an interface that is implemented by the Motorcycle class.

B. Vehicle and Motorcycle both implement the Transportation interface

C. Vehicle is a superclass of Motorcycle.

D. Motorcycle is a superclass of Vehicle.

E. Vehicle and Motorcycle both extend the Transportation superclass.

Answer: C, E

70. Given the code fragment:

```
public class Test {
    public static void main(String[] args) {
        /* insert code here */
        array[0]=10;
        array[1]=20;
        System.out.print(array[0]+":"+array[1]);
    }
}
```

Which code fragment, when inserted at line 3, enables the code to print 10:20?

A.
```
int[] array  = new int[1];
```

B.
```
int[] array;
array = new int[2];
```

C.
```
int array = new int[2];
```

D.
```
int array[1];
```

Answer: B

71. Given:

```
class Product {
    double price;
}

public class Test {
    public void updatePrice(Product product, double price) {
        price = price * 2;
        product.price = product.price + price;
    }
    public static void main(String[] args) {
        Product prt = new Product();
        prt.price = 200;
        double newPrice = 100;

        Test t = new Test();
        t.updatePrice(prt, newPrice);
        System.out.println(prt.price + " : " + newPrice);
    }
}
```

What is the result?

A. 200.0 : 100.0

B. 400.0 : 200.0

C. 400.0 : 100.0

D. Compilation fails.

Answer: C

72. Given these two classes:

```
public class Customer {
    ElectricAccount acct = new ElectricAccount();

    public void useElectricity(double kWh){
        acct.addKWh(kWh);
    }
}

public class ElectricAccount {
    private double kWh;
    private double rate = 0.07;
    private double bill;

    //line n1
}
```

Any amount of electricity used by a customer (represented by an instance of the Customer class)

must contribute to the customer's bill (represented by the member variable bill) through the

use Electricity method.

An instance of the Customer class should never be able to tamper with or decrease the value of

the member variable bill.

How should you write methods in the ElectricAccount class at line n1 so that the member variable

bill is always equal to the value of the member variable kwh multiplied by the member variable rate?

A.

```
public void addKWh(double kWh) {
    this.kWh += kWh;
    this.bill = this.kWh*this.rate;
}
```

B.

```
public void addKWh(double kWh) {
    if (kWh > 0){
        this.kWh += kWh;
        this.bill = this.kWh * this.rate;
    }
}
```

C.

```
private void addKWh(double kWh) {
    if (kWh > 0) {
        this.kWh += kWh;
        this.bill = this.kWh*this.rate;
    }
}
```

D.

```
public void addKWh(double kWh) {
    if(kWh > 0) {
        this.kWh += kWh;
        setBill(this.kWh);
    }
}
public void setBill(double kWh) {
    bill = kWh*rate;
}
```

Answer: A

73. Given the code fragment:

```
LocalDate date1 = LocalDate.now();
LocalDate date2 = LocalDate.of(6, 20, 2014 );
LocalDate date3 = LocalDate.parse("2014-06-20", DateTimeFormatter.ISO_DATE);
System.out.println("date1 = " + date1);
System.out.println("date2 = " + date2);
System.out.println("date3 = " + date3);
```

Assume that the system date is June 20, 2014. What is the result?

A.

```
date1 = 2014-06-20
date2 = 2014-06-20
date3 = 2014-06-20
```

B.

```
date1 = 06/20/2014
date2 = 2014-06-20
date3 = Jun 20, 2014
```

C. Compilation fails.

D. An exception is thrown at runtime.

Answer A

74. Given the code from the Greeting.Java file:

```
public class Greeting {
    public static void main(String[] args) {
        System.out.println("Hello " + args[0]);
    }
}
```

Which set of commands prints Hello Duke in the console?

```
A) javac Greeting
   java Greeting Duke

B) javac Greeting.java Duke
   java Greeting

C) javac Greeting.java
   java Greeting Duke

D) javac Greeting.java
   java Greeting.class Duke
```

A. Option A

B. Option B

C. Option C

D. Option D

Answer: C

75. Given:

```
class Vehicle {
    String type = "4W";
    int maxSpeed = 100;

    Vehicle(String type, int maxSpeed) {
        this.type = type;
        this.maxSpeed = maxSpeed;
    }
    Vehicle() {}
}

class Car extends Vehicle {
    String trans;

    Car(String trans) {           //line n1
        this.trans = trans;
    }

    Car(String type, int maxSpeed, String trans) {
        super(type, maxSpeed);    // line n2
        this.trans = trans;

    }
}
```

And given the code fragment:

```
Car c1 = new Car("Auto");
Car c2 = new Car("4W", 150, "Manual");
System.out.println(c1.type + " " + c1.maxSpeed + " " + c1.trans);
System.out.println(c2.type + " " + c2.maxSpeed + " " + c2.trans);
```

What is the result?

A. 4W 100 Auto 4W 150 Manual

B. null 0 Auto 4W 150 Manual

C. Compilation fails only at line n1

D. Compilation fails only at line n2

E. Compilation fails at both line n1 and line n2

Answer: E

76. Given the code fragment:

```
abstract class Planet {
    protected void revolve() {             //line n1
    }

    abstract void rotate();                //line n2
}

class Earth extends Planet {
    void revolve() {                       //line n3
    }

    protected void rotate() {              //line n4
    }
}
```

Which two modifications, made independently, enable the code to compile? (Choose two.)

A. Make the method at line n1 public.

B. Make the method at line n2 public.

C. Make the method at line n3 public.

D. Make the method at line n3 protected.

E. Make the method at line n4 public.

Answer: C, D

77. Given the following code:

```
public static void main(String[] args){
    String[] planets = {"Mercury", "Venus", "Earth", "Mars"};

    System.out.println(planets.length);
    System.out.println(planets[1].length());
}
```

What is the output?

A. 4

B. 3

C. 4

D. 5

E. 4

F. 4

Answer: E

78. Given:

```
interface Readable {
    public void readBook();
    public void setBookMark();
}

abstract class Book implements Readable {    // line n1
    public void readBook() { }
    // line n2
}

class EBook extends Book {                   // line n3
    public void readBook() { }
    // line n4
}
```

And given the code fragment:

Book book1 = new EBook();

book1.readBook();

Which option enables the code to compile?

A) Replace the code fragment at `line n1` with:
```
class Book implements Readable {
```

B) At `line n2` insert:
```
public abstract void setBookMark();
```

C) Replace the code fragment at `line n3` with:
```
abstract class EBook extends Book {
```

D) At `line n4` insert:
```
public void setBookMark() { }
```

A. Option A

B. Option B

C. Option C

D. Option D

Answer: D

79. Given:

```
System.out.println("5 + 2 = " + 3 + 4);
System.out.println("5 + 2 = " + (3 + 4));
```

What is the result?

```
A) 5 + 2 = 34
   5 + 2 = 34

B) 5 + 2 + 3 + 4
   5 + 2 = 7

C) 7 = 7
   7 + 7

D) 5 + 2 = 34
   5 + 2 = 7
```

A. Option A
B. Option B
C. Option C
D. Option D
Answer: D

80. Given the class definitions:

class C1 {}
class C2 extends C1 {}
class C3 extends C2 {}
and the code fragment:
C1 obj1 = (C1) new C2();
C2 obj2 = (C2) new C3();
C2 obj3 = (C2) new C1();
C3 obj4 = (C3) obj2;

Which line throws ClassCastException?

A. line 18
B. line 17
C. line 19
D. line 16
Answer: D

81.Given the code fragment:

```
int a[] = {1, 2, 3, 4, 5};
for(XXX) {
    System.out.print(a[e]);
}
```

Which option can replace xxx to enable the code to print 135?

A. int e = 0; e <= 4; e++
B. int e = 0; e < 5; e += 2
C. int e = 1; e <= 5; e += 1
D. int e = 1; e < 5; e+ =2

Answer: B

82. Which statement is true about the switch statement?

A. It must contain the default section.

B. The break statement, at the end of each case block, is optional.

C. Its case label literals can be changed at runtime.

D. Its expression must evaluate to a collection of values.

Answer: B

83. What will be the result of compiling and executing Test class?

```
public class Test {
  public static void main(String[] args) {
    Double [] arr = new Double[2];
    System.out.println(arr[0] + arr[1]);
  }
}
```

A. NullPointetExeeptian is thrown at runtime

B. 0.0

C. Compilation error

D. ClassCastException is thrown at runtime

Answer: A

84.Given the code fragment:

```
public static void main(String[] args) {
    Short s1 = 200;
    Integer s2 = 400;
    Long s3 = (long) s1 + s2;          //line n1
    String s4 = (String) (s3 * s2);    //line n2
    System.out.println("Sum is " + s4);
}
```

What is the result?

A. Sum is 600

B. Compilation fails at line n1.

C. Compilation fails at line n2.

D. A ClassCastException is thrown at line n1.

E. A ClassCastException is thrown at line n2.

Answer: C

85. Which statement best describes encapsulation?

A. Encapsulation ensures that classes can be designed so that only certain fields and methods of an object are accessible from other objects.

B. Encapsulation ensures that classes can be designed so that their methods are inheritable.

C. Encapsulation ensures that classes can be designed with some fields and methods declared as abstract.

D. Encapsulation ensures that classes can be designed so that if a method has an argument MyType x, any subclass of MyType can be passed to that method.

Answer: A

86. What is the name of the Java concept that uses access modifiers to protect variables and hide them within a class?

A. Encapsulation

B. Inheritance

C. Abstraction

D. Instantiation

E. Polymorphism

Answer: A

87. Given the code fragment:

```
String shirts[][] = new String[2][2];
shirts[0][0] = "red";
shirts[0][1] = "blue";
shirts[1][0] = "small";
shirts[1][1] = "medium";
```

Which code fragment prints red:blue:small:medium?

A.
```
for (int index = 1; index < 2; index++) {
    for (int idx = 1; idx < 2; idx++) {
        System.out.print(shirts[index][idx] + ":");
    }
}
```

B.
```
for (int index = 0; index < 2; ++index) {
    for (int idx = 0; idx < index; ++idx) {
        System.out.print(shirts[index][idx] + ":");
    }
}
```

C.
```
for (String [] c : shirts) {
    for (String s : c) {
        System.out.print(s + ":");
    }
}
```

D.
```
for (int index = 0; index <=2;) {
    for (int idx = 0; idx <=2;) {
        System.out.print(shirts[index][idx] + ":");
        idx++;
    }
    index++;
}
```

Answer: D

88. You are developing a banking module. You have developed a class named ccMask that has a maskcc method. Given the code fragment:

```
class CCMask {
    public static String maskCC(String creditCard) {
        String x = "XXXX-XXXX-XXXX-";
        //line n1
    }

    public static void main(String[] args) {
        System.out.println(maskCC("1234-5678-9101-1121"));
    }
}
```

You must ensure that the maskcc method returns a string that hides all digits of the credit card number except the four last digits (and the hyphens that separate each group of four digits). Which two code fragments should you use at line n 1, independently, to achieve this requirement? (Choose two.)

☐ A)
```
StringBuilder sb = new StringBuilder(creditCard);
sb.substring(15, 19);
return x + sb;
```

☐ B)
```
return x + creditCard.substring(15, 19);
```

☐ C)
```
StringBuilder sb = new StringBuilder(x);
sb.append(creditCard, 15, 19);
return sb.toString();
```

☐ D)
```
StringBuilder sb = new StringBuilder(creditCard);
StringBuilder s = sb.insert(0, x);
return s.toString();
```

A. Option A
B. Option B
C. Option C
D. Option D
Answer: B, C

89. Given the code fragment:

```
public static void main(String[] args) {
    StringBuilder sb = new StringBuilder("Java");
    String s = "Java";

    if (sb.toString().equals(s.toString()))  {
        System.out.println("Match 1");
    } else if (sb.equals(s)) {
        System.out.println("Match 2");
    } else {
        System.out.println("No Match");
    }
}
```

What is the result?

A. Match 1

B. Match 2

C. No Match

D. A NullPointerException is thrown at runtime.

Answer: A

90. Given the code fragment:

```
public class Test{

    void readCard(int cardNo) throws Exception {
        System.out.println("Reading Card");
    }

    void checkCard(int cardNo) throws RuntimeException { // line n1
        System.out.println("Checking Card");
    }

    public static void main(String[] args) {
        Test ex = new Test();
        int cardNo = 12344;
        ex.readCard(cardNo);                    //line n2
        ex.checkCard(cardNo);                   //line n3
    }
}
```

What is the result?

A.
```
Reading Card
Checking Card
```

B. Compilation fails only at line n1.

C. Compilation fails only at line n2.

D. Compilation fails only at line n3.

E. Compilation fails at both line n2 and line n3.

Answer: D

91. What will be the result of compiling and executing Test class?

```
import java.time.LocalTime;

public class Test {
  public static void main(String[] args) {
    LocalTime time = LocalTime.of(16, 40);
    String amPm = time.getHour() >= 12 ?
        (time.getHour() == 12) ? "PM" : "AM";
    System.out.println(amPm);
  }
}
```

A. PM

B. AM

C. Compilation error

D. An exception is thrown at runtime

Answer: C

92. What will be the result of compiling and executing Test class?

```
public class Test {
  public static void main(String[] args) {
    double [] arr = new int[2]; //Line 3
    System.out.println(arr[0]); //Line 4
  }
}
```

A. 0

B. 0.0

C. Line 3 causes compilation error

D. Line 4 causes runtime exception

Answer: C

93. Given the code fragment:

```
public static void main(String[] args) {
    Short s1 = 200;
    Integer s2 = 400;
    Long s3 = (long) s1 + s2;           //line n1
    String s4 = (String) (s3 * s2);     //line n2
    System.out.println("Sum is " + s4);
}
```

What is the result?

A. Sum is 600

B. Compilation fails at line nl.

C. Compilation fails at line n2.

D. A ClassCastException is thrown at line nl.

E. A ClassCastException is thrown at line n2.

Answer: C

94. What will be the result of compiling and executing Test class?

```
class Message {
  String msg = "Happy New Year!";

    public void print() {
    System.out.println(msg);
  }
}

public class Test {
  public static void change(Message m) {
    m = new Message();
    m.msg = "Happy Holidays!";
  }

    public static void main(String[] args) {
    Message obj = new Message();
    obj.print();
    change(obj);
    obj.print();
  }
}
```

A. Happy New Year;
Happy Holidays!

B. Happy Holidays!
Happy Holidays!

C. Happy New Year!
Happy New Year!

D. null
Happy New Year!

Answer: C

95. Consider the following class:

```
public class Employee {
  public int passportNo; //line 2
}
```

Which of the following is the correct way to make the variable 'passportNo’ read only for any other class?

A. Make 'PASSPORTNo’ private.

B. Make 'passportNo'private and provide a public method get PassportNo() which will return its value.

C. Ma 'passportNo' static and provide a public static method get PassportNo{}) which will return its value.

D. Remove ‘public' from the'passportNo' declaration. i.e., change line 2 to int passportNo;

Answer: B

96. What will be the result of compiling and executing Test class?

```
public class Test {
  public static void main(String[] args) {
    short [] args = new short[]{50, 50};
    args[0] = 5;
    args[1] = 10;
    System.out.println("[" + args[0] + ","
        + args[1] + "]");
  }
}
```

A. Compilation error

B. An thrown at runtime

C. [50, 50]

D. [5,10]

Answer. A

97. Which of these access modifiers can be used for a top level interface?

A. private

B. protected

C. public

D. All of the other options

Answer: C

98. Consider codes below:

```
//A.java
package com.udayan.oca;

public class A {
  public int i1 = 1;
  protected int i2 = 2;
}

//B.java
package com.udayan.oca.test;

        import com.udayan.oca.A;

public class B extends A {
  public void print() {
    A obj = new A();
    System.out.println(obj.i1); //Line 8
    System.out.println(obj.i2); //Line 9
    System.out.println(this.i2); //Line 10
    System.out.println(super.i2); //Line 11
  }

      public static void main(String [] args) {
    new B().print();
  }
}
```

One of the statements inside print() method is causing compilation failure. Which of the below solutions will help to resolve compilation error?

A. Comment the statement at Line 8

B. Comment the statement at Line 9

C. Comment the statement Line 10

D. Comment the statement at Line 11

Answer: B

99. Given:

```
class A {
    public A(){
        System.out.print("A ");
    }
}

class B extends A{
    public B(){                    //line n1
        System.out.print("B ");
    }
}

class C extends B{

    public C(){                    //line n2
        System.out.print("C ");
    }
    public static void main(String[] args) {
        C c = new C();
    }
}
```

What is the result?

A. C B A

B. C

C. A B C

D. Compilation fails at line n1 and line n2

Answer: C

100. Which statement is true about the switch statement?

A. It must contain the default section.

B. The break statement, at the end of each case block, is optional.

C. Its case label literals can be changed at runtime.

D. Its expression must evaluate to a collection of values.

Answer: B

Chapter 3 : The Oracle Certified Associate Java Programmer Part 3

101. What will be the result of compiling and executing Test class?

```
public class Test {
  public static void main(String[] args) {
    try {
      main(args);
    } catch (Exception ex) {
      System.out.println("CATCH-");
    }
    System.out.println("OUT");
  }
}
```

A. CATCH-OUT

B. OUT

C. None Of the System.out.println are executed

D Compilation error

Answer: C

102. Given:

```
class Product {
    double price;
}

public class Test {
    public void updatePrice(Product product, double price)
        price = price * 2;
        product.price = product.price + price;
    }
    public static void main(String[] args) {
        Product prt = new Product();
        prt.price = 200;
        double newPrice = 100;

        Test t = new Test();
        t.updatePrice(prt, newPrice);
        System.out.println(prt.price + " : " + newPrice);
    }
}
```

What is the result?

A. 200.0 : 100.0

B. 400.0 : 200.0

C. 400.0 : 100.0

D. Compilation fails.

Answer: C

103. Given this code for a Planet object:

```
public class Planet {
    public String name;
    public int moons;

    public Planet(String name, int moons) {
        this.name = name;
        this.moons = moons;
    }
}
```

And this method:

```
public static void main(String[] args){
    Planet[] planets = {
        new Planet("Mercury", 0),
        new Planet("Venus", 0),
        new Planet("Earth", 1),
        new Planet("Mars", 2)
    };

    System.out.println(planets);
    System.out.println(planets[2].name);
    System.out.println(planets[2].moons);
}
```

What is the output?

A.
```
planets
Earth
1
```

B.
```
[LPlanets.Planet;@15db9742
Earth
1
```

C.
```
[LPlanets.Planet;@15db9742
Planets.Planet@6d06d69c
1
```

D.
```
[LPlanets.Planet;@15db9742
Planets.Planet@6d06d69c
[LPlanets.Moon;@7852e922
```

E.
```
[LPlanets.Planet;@15db9742
Venus
0
```

Answer: C

104. Consider below code:

```
public class Test {
  public static void main(String[] args) {
    String str1 = new String("Core");
    String str2 = new String("CoRe");
    System.out.println(str1 = str2);
  }
}
```

What will be the result of compiling and executing Test class?

A. true

B. false

C. Core

D. CoRe

Answer: D

105.Given the code fragment

```
public class App {
    public static void main(String[] args) {
        String str1 = "Java";
        String str2 = new String("java");
        //line n1
        {
           System.out.println("Equal");
        } else {
           System.out.println("Not Equal");
        }
    }
}
```

Which code fragment, when inserted at line n1, enables the App class to print Equal?

```
A) Str 1.toLowerCase();
   if (str1 == str2)

B) if (str2.equals(str1.toLowerCase()))

C) Str 1.toLowerCase();
   if (str1.equals(str1.toLowerCase()))

D) if (str1.toLowerCase() == str2.toLowerCase())
```

A. Option A

B. Option B

C. Option C

D. Option D

Answer: B

106. Given the code fragment:

```
public static void main(String[] args) {
     int x = 6;
     while (isAvailable(x)) {
         System.out.print(x);

     }
}

public static boolean isAvailable(int x) {
    return --x > 0 ? true : false;
}
```

Which modification enables the code to print 54321?

A. Replace line 6 with System.out.print (--x);

B. At line 7, insert x --;

C. Replace line 5 with while (is Available(--x)) {

D. Replace line 12 with return (x > 0) ? false : true;

Answer: C

107. Given the following main method:

```
public static void main(String[] args) {
    int num = 5;
    do {
        System.out.print(num-- +" ");
    } while(num == 0);
}
```

What is the result?

A. 5 4 3 2 1 0

B. 5 4 3 2 1

C. 4 2 1

D. 5

E. Nothing is printed

Answer: D

108. Given

```
public class Test {

    public static void main(String[] args) {

        String[][] chs = new String[5][2];
        chs[0] = new String[2];
        chs[1] = new String[5];
        int i = 97;

        for (int a = 0; a < chs.length; a++) {
            for (int b = 0; b < chs.length; b++) {
                chs[a][b] = "" + i;
                i++;
            }
        }

        for (String[] ca : chs) {
            for (String c : ca) {
                System.out.print(c + " ");
            }
            System.out.println();
        }
    }
}
```

What is the result?

A. 97 98

99 100 null null null

B. 97 98

99 100 101 102 103

C. Compilation fails.

D. A NullPointerException is thrown at runtime.

E. An ArraylndexOutOfBoundsException is thrown at runtime.

Answer: E

109. Given the code fragment:

```
int[] array = {1, 2, 3, 4, 5};
```

And given the requirements:

1. Process all the elements of the array in the reverse order of entry.

2. Process all the elements of the array in the order of entry.

3. Process alternating elements of the array in the order of entry.

Which two statements are true? (Choose two.)

A. Requirements 1, 2, and 3 can be implemented by using the enhanced for loop.

B. Requirements 1, 2, and 3 can be implemented by using the standard for loop.

C. Requirements 2 and 3 CANNOT be implemented by using the standard for loop.

D. Requirement 2 can be implemented by using the enhanced for loop.

E. Requirement 3 CANNOT be implemented by using either the enhanced for loop or

the standard for loop

Answer: B, C

110. What is the name of the Java concept that uses access modifiers to protect variables and

hide them within a class?

A. Encapsulation

B. Inheritance

C. Abstraction

D. Instantiation

E. Polymorphism

Answer: A

111. Given the code snippet from a compiled Java source file:

```
public class MyFile
{
    public static void main (String[] args)
    {
        String arg1 = args[0];
        String arg2 = args[1];
        String arg3 = args[2];
        System.out.println("Arg is " + arg3);
    }
}
```

and this output:

```
Arg is 2
```

Which command should you run to obtain this output?

A. java MyFile 2

B. java MyFile 1 2 3 4

C. java MyFile 1 2 2

D. java MyFile 2 2

Answer: C

112. Which is true about the switch statement?

A. Its expression can evaluate to a collection of values.

B. The break statement, at the end of each case block, is optional.

C. Its case label literals can be changed at runtime.

D. It must contain the default section.

Answer: B

113.Which two modifications should you make so that the code compiles successfully?

(Choose two.)

A. Replace line 13 with:

```
try {
    xobj.printFileContent();
}
catch(Exception e) { }
catch(IOException e) { }
```

B. Replace line 7 with throw IOException ("Exception raised");

C. Replace line 11 with public static void main(String[]) args) throws Exception {

D. At line 14, insert throw new IOException();

E. Replace line 5 with public void printFileContent() throws IOException {

Answer: C, E

114. Given:

```
class Caller {
    private void init () {
        System.out.println("Initialized");
    }

    private void start () {
    init();
    System.out.println("Started");
    }
}

public class TestCall {
    public static void main(String[] args) {
        Caller c = new Caller();
        c.start(); // line n1
        c.init();  // line n2
    }
}
```

What is the result?

A. Compilation fails at line n1.

B. Initialized
Started
Initialized

C. Initialized
Started

D. Compilation fails at line n2

Answer: A

115. Given the code fragment:

```
public static void main(String[] args) {
    StringBuilder sb = new StringBuilder(5);
    String s = "";

    if (sb.equals(s)) {
        System.out.println("Match 1");
    } else if (sb.toString().equals(s.toString())) {
        System.out.println("Match 2");
    } else {
        System.out.println("No Match");
    }
}
```

What is the result?

A. Match 1

B. Match 2

C. No Match

D. A NullPointerException is thrown at runtime.

Answer: B

116. Given the code fragment:

```
public static void main(String[] args) {
    String date = LocalDate
                  .parse("2014-05-04")
                  .format(DateTimeFormatter.ISO_DATE_TIME);
    System.out.println(date);
}
```

What is the result?

A. May 04, 2014T00:00:00.000

B. 2014-05-04T00:00: 00.000

C. 5/4/14T00:00:00.000

D. An exception is thrown at runtime

Answer: D

117. Given the code fragment:

```
public static void main(String[] args) {
    StringBuilder sb = new StringBuilder("Java");
    String s = "Java";

    if (sb.toString().equals(s.toString()))  {
        System.out.println("Match 1");
    } else if (sb.equals(s)) {
        System.out.println("Match 2");
    } else {
        System.out.println("No Match");
    }
}
```

What is the result?

A. Match 1

B. Match 2

C. No Match

D. A NullPointerException is thrown at runtime.

Answer: A

118. Given:

```
class CD {
    int r;
    CD(int r){
        this.r=r;
    }
}

class DVD extends CD {
    int c;
    DVD(int r, int c) {
        // line n1
    }
}
```

And given the code fragment:

```
DVD dvd = new DVD(10,20);
```

Which code fragment should you use at line n1 to instantiate the dvd object successfully?

A)
```
super.r = r;
this.c = c;
```

B)
```
super(r);
this(c);
```

C)
```
super(r);
this.c = c;
```

D)
```
this.c = r;
super(c);
```

A. Option A
B. Option B
C. Option C
D. Option D
Answer: C

119. Given

```
interface Readable {
    public void readBook();
    public void setBookMark();
}

abstract class Book implements Readable {    // line n1
    public void readBook() { }
    // line n2
}

class EBook extends Book {                   // line n3
    public void readBook() { }
    // line n4
}
```

And given the code fragment:

Book book1 = new EBook ();

Book1.readBook();

Which option enables the code to compile?

- A) Replace the code fragment at `line n1` with:
  `class Book implements Readable {`
- B) At `line n2` insert:
  `public abstract void setBookMark();`
- C) Replace the code fragment at `line n3` with:
  `abstract class EBook extends Book {`
- D) At `line n4` insert:
  `public void setBookMark() { }`

A. Option A

B. Option B

C. Option C

D. Option D

Answer: D

120. Given the code fragment from three files:

SalesMan.java:

```
package sales;
public class SalesMan { }
```

Product.java:

```
package sales.products;
public class Product { }
```

Market.java:

```
1. package market;
2. // insert code here
3. public class USMarket {
4.     SalesMan sm;
5.     Product p;
6. }
```

Which code fragment, when inserted at line 2, enables the code to compile?

A) `import sales.*;`

B) `import java.sales.products.*;`

C)
```
import sales;
import sales.products;
```

D)
```
import sales.*;
import products.*;
```

E)
```
import sales.*;
import sales.products.*;
```

A. Option A
B. Option B
C. Option C
D. Option D
E. Option E

Answer: E

121. Given the code fragment:

```
int x = 100;
int a = x++;
int b = ++x;
int c = x++;
int d = (a < b) ? (a < c) ? a: (b <c )? b: c: x;
System.out.println(d);
```

What is the result?

A. 100
B. 101
C. 102
D. 103
E. Compilation fails

Answer: A

122. Given

```
class X {
    static int i;
    int j;
    public static void main(String[] args) {
        X x1 = new X();
        X x2 = new X();
        x1.i = 3;
        x1.j = 4;
        x2.i = 5;
        x2.j = 6;
        System.out.println(
            x1.i + " " +
            x1.j + " " +
            x2.i + " " +
            x2.j);
    }
}
```

What is the result?

A. 3 4 5 6

B. 3 4 3 6

C. 5 4 5 6

D. 3 6 4 6

Answer: C

123. Given the code fragment:

```
public static void main(String[] args) {
    List<String> names = new ArrayList<>();
    names.add("Robb");
    names.add("Bran");
    names.add("Rick");
    names.add("Bran");

    if (names.remove("Bran")) {
        names.remove("Jon");
    }
    System.out.println(names);
}
```

What is the result?

A. [Robb, Rick, Bran]

B. [Robb, Rick]

C. [Robb, Bran, Rick, Bran]

D. An exception is thrown at runtime.

Answer: A

124. Given the code fragment:

```
public class Employee {
    String name;
    boolean contract;
    double salary;
    Employee() {
        // line n1
    }
    public String toString(){
        return name + ":" + contract + ":" + salary;
    }
    public static void main(String[] args) {
        Employee e = new Employee();
        // line n2
        System.out.print(e);
    }
}
```

Which two modifications, when made independently, enable the code to print joe:true: 100.0? (Choose two.)

☐ A) Replace `line n2` with:

```
e.name = "Joe";
e.contract = true;
e.salary = 100;
```

☐ B) Replace `line n2` with:

```
this.name = "Joe";
this.contract = true;
this.salary = 100;
```

☐ C) Replace `line n1` with:

```
this.name = new String("Joe");
this.contract = new Boolean(true);
this.salary = new Double(100);
```

☐ D) Replace `line n1` with:

```
name = "Joe";
contract = TRUE;
salary = 100.0f;
```

☐ E) Replace `line n1` with:

```
this("Joe", true, 100);
```

A. Option A
B. Option B
C. Option C
D. Option D
E. Option E
Answer: A, C

125. Given the code fragment:

```
public static void main(String[] args) {
    String[] arr = {"A", "B", "C", "D"};
    for (int i = 0; i < arr.length; i++) {
        System.out.print(arr[i] + " ");
        if (arr[i].equals("C")) {
            continue;
        }
        System.out.println("Work done");
        break;
    }
}
```

What is the result?

A. A B C Work done

B. A B C D Work done

C. A Work done

D. Compilation fails

Answer: C

126. Given the code fragment:

```
public static void main(String[] args) {
    double discount = 0;
    int qty = Integer.parseInt(args[0]);
    //line n1;
}
```

And given the requirements:

If the value of the qty variable is greater than or equal to 90, discount = 0.5

If the value of the qty variable is between 80 and 90, discount = 0.2

Which two code fragments can be independently placed at line n1 to meet the requirements? (Choose two.)

```
☐ A) if (qty >= 90) { discount = 0.5; }
     if (qty > 80 && qty < 90) { discount = 0.2; }

☐ B) discount = (qty >= 90) ? 0.5 : 0;
     discount = (qty > 80) ? 0.2 : 0;

☐ C) discount = (qty >= 90) ? 0.5 : (qty > 80)? 0.2 : 0;

☐ D) if (qty > 80 && qty < 90) {
         discount = 0.2;
     } else {
         discount = 0;
     }
     if (qty >= 90) {
         discount = 0.5;
     } else {
         discount = 0;
     }

☐ E) discount = (qty > 80) ? 0.2 : (qty >= 90) ? 0.5 : 0;
```

A. Option A

B. Option B

C. Option C

D. Option D

E. Option E

Answer: A, C

127. Given the code fragment

```
LocalDate date1 = LocalDate.now();
LocalDate date2 = LocalDate.of(2014, 6, 20);
LocalDate date3 = LocalDate.parse("2014-06-20", DateTimeFormatter.ISO_DATE);
System.out.println("date1 = " + date1);
System.out.println("date2 = " + date2);
System.out.println("date3 = " + date3);
```

Assume that the system date is June 20, 2014. What is the result?

A.
```
date1 = 2014-06-20
date2 = 2014-06-20
date3 = 2014-06-20
```

B.
```
date1 = 06/20/2014
date2 = 2014-06-20
date3 = Jun 20, 2014
```

C. Compilation fails.

D. A `DateParseException` is thrown at runtime.

Answer: A

128. Given the definitions of the MyString class and the Test class:

MyString.java:

```
package p1;
class MyString {
    String msg;
    MyString(String msg) {
        this.msg = msg;
    }
}
```

Test.java:

```
package p1;
public class Test {
    public static void main(String[] args) {
        System.out.println("Hello " + new StringBuilder("Java SE 8"));
        System.out.println("Hello " + new MyString("Java SE 8"));
    }
}
```

What is the result?

A.
```
Hello Java SE 8
Hello Java SE 8
```

B.
```
Hello java.lang.StringBuilder@<<hashcode1>>
Hello p1.MyString@<<hashcode2>>
```

C.
```
Hello Java SE 8
Hello p1.MyString@<<hashcode>>
```

D. Compilation fails at the Test class

Answer: C

129. Which three statements describe the object-oriented features of the Java language?

(Choose three)

A. Objects cannot be reused.

B. A subclass can inherit from a superclass.

C. Objects can share behaviors with other objects.

D. A package must contain more than one class.

E. Object is the root class of all other objects.

F. A main method must be declared in every class.

Answer: B, C

130. Given

Base.java:

```
class Base {
    public void test(){
        System.out.println("Base ");
    }
}
```

DerivedA.java:

```
class DerivedA extends Base {
    public void test(){
        System.out.println("DerivedA ");
    }
}
```

DerivedB.java:

```
class DerivedB  extends DerivedA {
    public void test(){
        System.out.println("DerivedB ");
    }
    public static void main(String[] args) {
        Base b1 = new DerivedB();
        Base b2 = new DerivedA();
        Base b3 = new DerivedB();
        b1 = (Base) b3;
        Base b4 = (DerivedA) b3;
        b1.test();
        b4.test();
    }
}
```

What is the result?

A. Base
DerivedA

B. Base
DerivedB

C. DerivedB
DerivedB

D. DerivedB
DerivedA

E. A ClassCastException is thrown at runtime.

Answer: C

131. You are asked to develop a program for a application and you are given this information:

- The application must contain he classes Toy, EduToy, and ConsToy. The Toy class is the superclass of the other two classes
- The int calculatePrice (Toy t) method calculates the price of a toy.
- The void printToy (Toy t) methods prints the details of a toy.

Which definition of the Toy class adds a valid layer of abstraction to the class hierarchy?

```
A. public abstract class Toy{
       public abstract int calculatePrice(Toy t);
       public void printToy(Toy t) { /* code goes here */ }
   }

B. public abstract class Toy {
       public int calculatePrice(Toy t) ;
       public void printToy(Toy t) ;
   }

C. public abstract class Toy {
       public int calculatePrice(Toy t);
       public final void printToy(Toy t){ /* code goes here */ }
   }

D. public abstract class Toy {
       public abstract int calculatePrice(Toy t) { /* code goes here */ }
       public abstract void printToy(Toy t) { /* code goes here */ }
   }
```

Answer: A

132. Given the following code

```
int[] intArr = {15, 30, 45, 60, 75};
intArr[2] = intArr[4];
intArr[4] = 90;
```

What are the values of each element in intArr after this code has executed?

A. 15, 60, 45, 90, 75

B. 15, 90, 45, 90, 75

C. 15, 30, 75, 60, 90

D. 15, 30, 90, 60, 90

E. 15, 4, 45, 60, 90

Answer: C

133. Given the content of three files:

```
A.java:

public class A {
    public void a() {}
    int a;
}

B.java:

public class B {
    private int doStuff() {
        private int x = 100;
        return x++;
    }
}

C.java:

import java.io.*;
package p1;
class A {
    public void main(String fileName) throws IOException { }
}
```

Which statement is true?

A. Only the A.Java file compiles successfully.

B. Only the B.java file compiles successfully.

C. Only the C.java file compiles successfully.

D. The A.Java and B.java files compile successfully.

E. The B.java and C.java files compile successfully.

F. The A.Java and C.java files compile successfully.

Answer: A

134. Which statement is true about Java byte code?

A. It can run on any platform.

B. It can run on any platform only if it was compiled for that platform.

C. It can run on any platform that has the Java Runtime Environment.

D. It can run on any platform that has a Java compiler. Given the code.

It can run on any platform only if that platform has both the Java Runtime Environment and

a Java compiler.

Answer: D

135. Given:

```
public class Triangle {
    static double area;
    int b = 2, h = 3;
    public static void main(String[] args) {
        double p, b, h;          //line n1
        if (area == 0) {
            b = 3;
            h = 4;
            p = 0.5;
        }
        area = p * b * h;        //line n2
        System.out.println("Area is " + area);
    }
}
```

What is the result?

A. Area is 6.0

B. Area is 3.0

C. Compilation fails at line n1

D. Compilation fails at line n2.

Answer: D

136. Given

```
public class Vowel {
    private char var;
    public static void main(String[] args) {
        char var1 = 'a';
        char var2 = var1;
        var2 = 'e';

        Vowel obj1 = new Vowel();
        Vowel obj2 = obj1;
        obj1.var = 'o';
        obj2.var = 'i';

       System.out.println(var1 + ", " +var2);
       System.out.print(obj1.var + ", " + obj2.var);
    }
}
```

What is the result?

A. a, e
i, i

B. a, e
o, o

C. e, e
i, i

D. a, a
o, o

Answer: A

137.Given the code fragment

```
public class Test {
    public static void main(String[] args) {
        //line n1
        switch (x) {
            case 1:
                System.out.println("One");
                break;
            case 2:
                System.out.println("Two");
                break;
        }
    }
}
```

Which three code fragments can be independently inserted at line n1 to enable the code to print one? (Choose three.)

A. Byte x = 1;

B. short x = 1;

C. String x = "1";

D. Long x = 1;

E. Double x = 1;

F. Integer x = new Integer ("1");

Answer: A, B, F

138. Which two are benefits of polymorphism? (Choose two.)

A. Faster code at runtime

B. More efficient code at runtime

C. More dynamic code at runtime

D. More flexible and reusable code

E.Code that is protected from extension by other classes

Answer: B, D

139.Given the code fragment: Boolean bl =true Boolean b2 =false; int i = 0; while (foo) { }

Which one is valid as a replacement for foo?

A. b1.compareTo(b2)

B. i=1

C. i = =2?-1 : 0

D. "foo"

Answer: D

140. Given the following classes:

```
public class Employee {
    public int salary;
}

public class Manager extends Employee {
    public int budget;
}

public class Director extends Manager {
    public int stockOptions;
}
```

And given the following `main` method:

```
public static void main(String[] args) {
    Employee employee = new Employee();
    Manager  manager  = new Manager();
    Director director = new Director();
    //line n1
}
```

Which two options fail to compile when placed at line n1 of the main method? (Choose two.)

A. employee.salary = 50_000;

B. director.salary = 80_000;

C. employee.budget = 200_000;

D. manager.budget = 1_000_000;

E. manager.stockOption = 500;

F. director.stockOptions = 1_000;

Answer: C,E

141.Which statement will empty the contents of a StringBuilder variable named sb?

A. sb. deleteAll ();

B. sb. delete (0, sb. size ());

C. sb. delete (0, sb. length ());

D. sb. removeAll ();

Answer: C

142.

Class A {}Class B {}

Interface X {} Interface Y {}

Which two definitions of class C are valid?

A. Class C extends A implements X {}

B. Class C implements extends B {}

C. Class C extends A, B {}

D Class C implements X, Y extends B{}

E. Class C extends B implements X, Y{}

Answer. A, E

143. Given the code fragment:

```
int a[] = {1, 2, 3, 4, 5};
for(XXX) {
    System.out.print(a[e]);
}
```

Which option can replace xxx to enable the code to print 135?

A. int e = 0; e < = 4; e++

B. int e = 0; e < 5; e + = 2

C. int e = 1; e < = 5; e + = 1

D. int e = 1; e < 5; e+ =2

Answer: D

144. Given:

```
class Patient {
    String name;
    public Patient (String name) {
        this.name = name;
    }
}
```

And the code fragment

```
public class Test {
    public static void main (String [] args) {
       List ps = new ArrayList ();
       Patient p2 = new Patient ("Mike);
       ps.add(p2);

       // insert code here

       if (f >= 0) {
           System.out.print ("Mike Found");
       }
    }
}
```

Which code fragment, when inserted at line 14, enables the code to print Mike Found?

A. `int f = ps.indexOf (p2);`

B. `int f = ps.indexOf (Patient ("Mike") );`

C. `int f = ps.indexOf (new Patient "Mike") );`

D.
```
Patient p = new Patient ("Mike");
Int f = ps.indexOf (p)
```

Answer: A

145. Given the code fragment:

System-out.println ("Result:"3 + 5); System.out.println ("Result: + (3 + 5));

What the result?

A. Result: 8 Result: **8**

B. Result: 35 Result:**8**

C. Result: 8 Result: 3**5**

D. Result: 35 Result: 35

Answer: B

146. Given the code fragment:

```
if (aVar++ < 10) {
    System.out.println(aVar + " Hello Universe!");
} else {
    System.out.println(aVar + " Hello World!");
}
```

What is the result if the integer aVar is 9?

A. Compilation fails.

B. 10 Hello Universe!

C. 10 Hello World!

D. 9 Hello World!

Answer: B

147. Given the code fragment:

```
public static void main(String[] args) {
    int[][] arr = new int [2] [4];
    arr[0] = new int []{1, 3, 5, 7};
    arr[1] = new int []{1, 3};
    for (int[] a : arr) {
        for (int i : a) {
            System.out.print(i+ " ");
        }
        System.out.println();
    }
}
```

What is the result?

A. Compilation fails.

B. 1 3
1 3

C. 1 3
followed by an Array Index Out Of Bounds Exception

D. 1 3
1 3 0 0

E. 1 3 5 7
1 3

Answer: E

148. Given the following class

```
public class CheckingAccount {
    public int amount;
    public CheckingAccount(int amount){
        this.amount = amount;
    }
    public int getAmount(){
        return amount;
    }
    public void changeAmount(int x){
        amount += x;
    }
}
```

And given the following main method, located in another class:

```
public static void main(String[] args) {
    CheckingAccount acct = new CheckingAccount((int)(Math.random()*100
    //line n1
    System.out.println(acct.getAmount());
}
```

Which three lines, when inserted independently at line n1, cause the program to print a o balance?

A. this.amount = 0;

B. amount = 0;

C. acct (0) ;

D. acct.amount = 0;

E. acct. getAmount () = 0;

F. acct.changeAmount(0);

G. acct.changeAmount(-acct.amount);

H. acct.changeAmount(-acct.getAmount());

Answer: A, C, D

149. Which two statements are true for a two-dimensional array?

A. It is implemented as an array Of the specified element type-

B. Using a row by column convention, each row of a two-dimensional array must be ofthe same size.

C. At declaration time, the number of elements of the array in each dimension must be specified.

D All methods of the class Object may be invoked on the two-dimensional array.

Answer: A, D

150. What is the result of the following program?

```
public class MathFunctions {
  public static void addToInt(int x, int amountToAdd) {
    x = x + amountToAdd;
  }

 public static void main(String[] args) {
   int a = 15;
   int b = 10;
   MathFunctions.addToInt(a, b);
   System.out.println(a);    } }
```

A. 10

B. 15

C. 25

D. Compiler error on line 3.

E. Compiler error on line 8.

F. None of the above.

Answer: B.

151: You are asked to create a method that accepts an array of integers and returns the highest value from that array.

Given the code fragment:

```
class Test {
    public static void main (String [] args) {
        int numbers [] = {12, 13, 42, 32, 15, 156, 23, 51, 12};
        int max = findMax (numbers);
}
/*line n1 */ {
   int max = 0;
   /* code goes here*/
   return max;
 }
}
```

Which method signature do you use at line n1?

A. public int findMax (int [] numbers)

B. static int[] findMax (int max)

C. static int findMax (int [] numbers)

D. final int findMax (int [])

Answer: A

152. Given the code fragment

```
public class Test {

    static int count = 0;
    int i = 0;

    public void changeCount() {
        while (i < 5) {
            i++;
            count++;
        }
    }

    public static void main(String[] args) {
        Test check1 = new Test();
        Test check2 = new Test();
        check1.changeCount();
        check2.changeCount();
        System.out.print(check1.count + " : " + check2.count);
    }
}
```

What is the result?

A. 10 : 10

B. 5 : 5

C. 5 : 10

D. Compilation fails

Answer: C

153. Given the code fragment:

```
float var1 = (12_345.01 <= 123_45.00) ? 12_456 : 124_56.02f;
float var2 = var1 + 1024;
System.out.print(var2);
```

What is the result?

A. An exception is thrown at runtime.

B. Compilation fails.

C. 13480.0

D. 13480.02

Answer: D

154. What is the output of the following program?

```
public class FeedingSchedule {
 public static void main(String[] args) {
   boolean keepGoing = true;
   int count = 0;
   int x = 3;
   while(count++ < 3) {
     int y = (1 + 2 * count) % 3;
     switch(y) {
        default:
         case 0: x -= 1; break;
         case 1: x += 5;
     }
   }
  System.out.println(x);
 } }
```

A. 4

B.5

C. 6

D. 7

E. 13

F. The code will not compile because of line 7.

Answer: C

155. Which two statements correctly describe checked exception?

A. These are exceptional conditions that a well-written application should anticipate and
recover from

B. These Are exceptional conditions that are external to the Application, and the application
usually cannot anticipate or recover from.

C. These are exceptional conditions that are internal to the application. and that the
application usually cannot anticipate or recover from.

D. Every class that is a subclass Of RuntimeException and Error is categorized as
checked exception-

E. Every class that is a subclass of Exception, excluding RuntimeException and its subclasses
is categorized as checked exception.

Answer: B, D

156. Given:

```
public class App {
    int count;
    public static void displayMsg () {
        count++;                                        // line n1
    System.out.println ("Welcome "+"Visit Count: "+count); // line n2
    }
    public static void main (String [] args) {
        App.displayMsg ();                              // line n3
        App.displayMsg ();                              // line n4
    }
}
```

What is the result ?

A. Compilation fails at line n3 and line n4.

B. Compilation fails at line n1 and line n2.

C. Welcome Visit Count:1
Welcome Visit Count: 1

D. Welcome Visit Count:1
Welcome Visit Count: 2

Answer: B

157. Given the code fragments:

Person.java:

```
public class Person {
    String name;
    int age;

    public Person(String n, int a) {
        name = n;
        age = a;
    }

    public String getName() {
        return name;
    }

    public int getAge() {
        return age;
    }
}
```

Test.java:

```
public static void checkAge(List<Person> list, Predicate<Person> predic
    for (Person p : list) {
        if (predicate.test(p)) {
            System.out.println(p.name + " ");
        }
    }
}

public static void main(String[] args) {
    List<Person> iList = Arrays.asList(new Person("Hank", 45),
                                       new Person("Charlie", 40),
                                       new Person("Smith", 38));
    //line n1
}
```

Which code fragment, when inserted at line n1, enables the code to print Hank?

A. checkAge (iList, ( ) -> p. get Age ( ) > 40);

B. checkAge(iList, Person p -> p.getAge( ) > 40);

C. checkAge (iList, p -> p.getAge ( ) > 40);

D. checkAge(iList, (Person p) -> { p.getAge() > 40; }) ;

Answer: D

158.

```
class Test {
   public static void main (String [] args) {
        int numbers [ ];
        numbers = new int [2];
        numbers [0] = 10;
        numbers [1] = 20;

        numbers = new int [4];
        numbers [2] = 30;
        numbers [3] = 40;
        for (int x : numbers) {
            System.out.print (" " + x) ;
        }
   }
}
```

What is the result?

A. 10 20 30 40

B. 0 0 30 40

C. Compilation fails.

D. An exception is thrown at runtime.

Answer: C

159. Given the code fragments

```
class Student {
     String name;
     int age;
}
```

And:

```
public class Test {
  public static void main(String[] args) {
       Student s1 = new Student();
       Student s2 = new Student();
       Student s3 = new Student();
       s1 = s3;
       s3 = s2;
       s2 = null;
  }
}
```

Which statement is true?

A. After line 11, three objects are eligible for garbage collection.

B. After line 11, two objects are eligible for garbage collection.

C. After line 11, one object is eligible for garbage collection.

D. After line 11, none of the objects are eligible for garbage collection.

Answer: C

160.Given the code fragment:

```
public static void main (String [] args) {
    String myStr = "Hello World";
    myStr.trim ()
    int i1 = myStr.indexOf (" ");
    System.out.printLn (i1);
}
```

What is the result?

A. An exception is thrown at runtime.

B. -1

C. 5

D. 0

Answer: A

161. What is the result of the following code?

```
int[] array = {6,9,8};

List<Integer> list = new ArrayList<>();
list.add(array[0]);
list.add(array[2]);
list.set(1, array[1]);
list.remove(0);
System.out.println(list);
```

A. [8]

B. [9]

C. Something like **[Ljava.lang.String; @160bc7c0**

D. An exception is thrown.

E. The code does not compile.

Answer: B

162. Given the code fragment:

```
public class Person {
    String name;
    int age = 25;

    public Person(String name) {
        this();                             //line n1
        setName(name);
    }

    public Person(String name, int age) {
        Person(name);                       //line n2
        setAge(age);
    }

    //setter and getter methods go here

    public String show() {
        return name + " " + age + " " + number ;
    }
    public static void main(String[] args) {
        Person p1 = new Person("Jesse");
        Person p2 = new Person("Walter",52);
        System.out.println(p1.show());
        System.out.println(p2.show());
    }
}
```

What is the result?

A. Jesse 25

Walter 52

B. Compilation fails only at line n1

C. Compilation fails only at line n2

D. Compilation fails at both line n1 and line n2

Answer: B

163.Given the code fragment

```
public static void main (String[ ] args) {
    int data [] = {2010, 2013, 2014, 2015, 2014};
    int key = 2014;
    int count = 0;
    for (int e: data) {
         if (e! = key) {
             continue:
             count++;
         }
    }
    System.out.print (count + "Found");
}
```

What is the result?

A. Compilation fails.

B. 0 Found

C. 1 Found

D. 3 Found

Answer: C

164. Given the code fragment:

```
public static void main(String[] args) {
     LocalDate date = LocalDate.of(2012, 01, 32);
     date.plusDays(10);
     System.out.println(date);
}
```

What is the result?

A. 2012-02-10

B. 2012-02-11

C. Compilation fails

D. A DateTimeException is thrown at runtime.

Answer: D

165. Given the code fragment

```
LocalDate Time dt= LocalDateTime.of (2014, 7, 31, 1, 1);
dt.plusDays (30);
dt. plusMonths (1);
System.out.print (dt format (DateTimeFormatter. ISO_DATE) );
```

What is the result?

A. An exception is thrown at runtime.

B. 07-31-2014

C. 2014-07-31

D. 2014-09-30

Answer: C

166. What is the output of the following code?

```
public class Deer {
 public Deer() { System.out.print("Deer"); }

public Deer(int age) { System.out.print("DeerAge"); }
private boolean hasHorns() { return false; }
public static void main(String[] args) {
  Deer deer = new Reindeer(5);
  System.out.println(","+deer.hasHorns());
}
}
class Reindeer extends Deer {
 public Reindeer(int age) { System.out.print("Reindeer");

 public boolean hasHorns() { return true; }
}
```

A. DeerReindeer,false

B. DeerReindeer,true

C. ReindeerDeer,false

D. ReindeerDeer,true

E. DeerAgeReindeer,false

F. DeerAgeReindeer,true

G. The code will not compile because of line 7.

H. The code will not compile because of line 12.

Answer: A

167. Given:

```
public class Test {
      public static int stVar = 100;
      public int var = 200;
      public String toString() {
            return var + ":" + stVar;
      }
}
```

And given the code fragment:

```
Test t1 = new Test();
t1.var = 300;
System.out.println(t1);
Test t2 = new Test();
t2.stVar = 300;
System.out.println(t2);
```

What is the result?

A. 300:300
200:300

B. 300:100
200:300

C. 300:0
0:300

D. 200:300
200:300

168. Given:

```
public class App {
    public static void main(String[] args) {
        int i = 10;
        int j = 20;
        int k =(j += i)/ 5;
        System.out.print(i + " : " + j + " : " + k);
    }
}
```

What is the result?

A. 10 : 30 : 6

B. 10 : 22 : 22

C. 10 : 22 : 20

D. 10 : 22 : 6

Answer: A

169. Given

```
class C2 {
    public void displayC2() {
        System.out.print("C2");
    }
}
interface I {
    public void displayI();
}
class C1 extends C2 implements I {
    public void displayI() {
        System.out.print("C1");
    }
}
```

And given the code fragment:

```
C2 obj1 = new C1();
I obj2 = new C1();

C2 s = obj2;
I t = obj1;

t.displayI();
s.displayC2()
```

What is the result?

A. C2C2

B. C1C2

C. C1C1

D. Compilation fails

Answer: B

170. Which of the following statements are true? (Choose all that apply)

A. Checked exceptions are intended to be thrown by the JVM(and not the programmer).

B. Checked exceptions are required to be caught or declared.

C. Errors are intended to be thrown by the JVM (and not theprogrammer).

D. Errors are required to be caught or declared.

H. Runtime exceptions are intended to be thrown by the JVM(and not the programmer).

I. Runtime exceptions are required to be caught or declared.

Answer: B, C.

171.Which two are valid declarations of a two-dimensional array?

A. int[][] array2D;

B. int [2][2] array2D;

C. int array2D

D. int [] [];

E. int [][] array2D[];

Answer- A, D

172. Given

```
interface Downloadable {
      public void download();
}

interface Readable extends Downloadable {          // line n1
      public void readBook();
}

abstract class Book implements Readable {          // line n2
      public void readBook() {
            System.out.println("Read Book");
      }
}

class EBook extends Book {                         // line n3
      public void readBook() {
            System.out.println("Read E-Book");
      }
}
```

And given the code fragment:

```
Book book1 = new EBook();
book1.readBook();
```

What is the result?

A. Compilation fails at line n2.

B. Read Book

C. Read E-Book

D. Compilation fails at line n1.

E. Compilation fails at line n3.

Answer: E

173.Given the code fragment:

```
List colors = new ArrayList();
colors.add("green");
colors.add("red");
colors.add("blue");
colors.add("yellow");
colors.remove(2);
colors.add(3, "cyan");
System.out.print(colors);
```

What is the result?

A. (green, red, yellow, cyan)

B. (green, blue, yellow, cyan)

C. (green, red, cyan, yellow)

D. An IndexOutOfBoundsException is thrown at runtime.

Answer: C

174. Which statement is true about the default constructor of a top-level class?

A. It can take arguments.

B. It has private access modifier in its declaration.

C. It can be overloaded.

D. The default constructor of a subclass always invokes the no-argument constructor of its

superclass.

Answer: D

175. Given the code fragment:

int b = 3;

if((b>3))

{System .out.println("square");

}{

System.out.println("circle");

}

System.out.println(".,."); What is the result?

A. square

B. circle.

C. squarecircle

D. Compilation fails.

Answer- C

176. Given this class:

```
public class Rectangle {
      private double length;
      private double height;
      private double area;

      public void setLength(double length) {
            this.length = length;
      }
      public void setHeight(double height) {
            this.height = height;
      }
      public void setArea() {
            area = length*height;
      }
}
```

Which two changes would encapsulate this class and ensure that the area field is always equal to length * height whenever the Rectangle class is used?

A. Call the setArea method at the end of the setHeight method.

B. Call the setArea method at the beginning of the setHeight method.

C. Call the setArea method at the end of the setLength method.

D. Call the setArea method at the beginning of the setLength method.

E. Change the setArea method to private.

F. Change the area field to public.

Answer: A,C

177. What is the proper way to defined a method that take two int values and returns their sum

as an int value?

A. int sum(int first, int second) { first + second; }

B. int sum(int first. second) (return first + second;

C. sum(int first, int second) (return first

second;)

D. int sum(int first, int second) { return first second; E. void sum (int first, int second)

return first second;

Answer: D

178. Given:

```
class Test
    int a1;

    public static void doProduct(int a) {
        a = a * a;
    }

    public static void doString(String s) {
        s.concat(" " + s);
    }

    public static void main(String[] args) {
        Test item = new Test();
        item.a1 = 11;
        String sb = "Hello";
        Integer i = 10;
        doProduct(i);
        doString(sb);
        doProduct(item.a1);
        System.out.println(i + " " + sb + " " + item.a1);
    }
}
```

What is the result?

A. 10 Hello Hello 11

B. 10 Hello Hello 121

C. 100 Hello 121

D. 100 Hello Hello 121

E. 10 Hello 11

Answer: E

179. Which of the following can fill in the blank in this code to make it compile? (Select 2 options.)

```
public void method()_____Exception {
________Exception();
}
```

A. On line 1, fill in throws

B. On line 1, fill in throws new

C. On line 2, fill in throw new

D. On line 2, fill in throws

E. On line 2, fill in throws new

Answer: A, C

180. Which two are Java Exception classes?

A. SercurityException

B. DuplicatePathExceptian

C. IllegalArgumentException

D. TooManyArgumentsException

Answer: A, C

181: Which three Statements true about the Structure Of a JAVA Class? (Choose three.)

A. class cannot have the same name as its field.

B. A public class must have a main method.

C. A class can have final static methods.

D. A can overloaded private constructors.

E. Fields need to be initialized before use.

F. Methods and fields are optional components of a class.

Answer: B, D, E

182: Given a java source file: What changes will make this code compile? (Select Two)

A. Adding the public modifier to the declaration of class

B. Adding the protected modifier to the x() constructor

C. Changing the private modifier on the declaration Of the one() method to protected

D. Removing the Y() constructor

E. Removing the private modifier from the two() method

Answer: C, E

183: Given:

```
class Student {
      String name;
      public Student(String name) {
            this.name = name;
      }
}

public class Test {
      public static void main(String[] args) {
            Student[] students = new Student[3];
            students[1] = new Student("Richard");
            students[2] = new Student("Donald");
            for (Student s : students) {
                  System.out.println("" + s.name);
            }
      }
}
```

What is the result?

A. null
Richard
Donald

B. Richard
Donald

C. Compilation fails.

D. An ArrayIndexOutOfBoundsException is thrown at runtime.

E. A NullPointerException is thrown at runtime.

184:

```
public class FieldInit {
    Character c;
    boolean b;
    float f;
    void printAll() {
        System.out.println("c = " + c);
        System.out.println("b = " + b);
        System.out.println("f = " + f);
    }

    public static void main(String[] args) {
        FieldInit f = new FieldInit();
        f.printAll();
    }
}
```

What is the result?

```
c =
b = false
f = 0.0
```
A.

```
c = null
b = true
f = 0.0
```
B.

```
c = 0
b = false
f = 0.0F
```
C.

```
c = null
b = false
f = 0.0
```
D.

Answer: D

185. Given the code fragment:

```
int n[][] = {{1, 3}, {2, 4}};
for (int i = n.length - 1; i >= 0; i--) {
    for (int j = n[i].length - 1; j >= 0; j--) {
        System.out.print(n[i][j]);
    }
}
```

What is the result?

A. 3142

B. 2413

C. 1324

D. 4231

Answer: D

186. What is the result?

A. Null

B. Compilation fails

C. An exception is thrown at runtime

D. 0

Answer: C

187. Which are true of the following code? (Choose all that apply)

```
import java.util.*;
public class Grasshopper {
public Grasshopper(String n) {
   name = n;
}
public static void main(String[] args) {
  Grasshopper one = new Grasshopper("g1");
  Grasshopper two = new Grasshopper("g2");
  one = two;
  two = null;
  one = null;

 }
   private String name; }
```

A. Immediately after line 9, no grasshopper objects areeligible for garbage collection.

B. Immediately after line 10, no grasshopper objects areeligible for garbage collection.

C. Immediately after line 9, only one grasshopper object iseligible for garbage collection.

D. Immediately after line 10, only one grasshopper object iseligible for garbage collection.

E. Immediately after line 11, only one grasshopper object iseligible for garbage collection.

F. The code compiles.

G. The code does not compile.

Answer: C, D, F.

188. Which of the following exception will be thrown due to the statement given here?

int array[]= new int[-2];

A. NullPointerException

B. NegativeArraySizeExeeption

C. Array**Index**OutOfBoundsException

D. IndexOutOfBoundsE**xception**

E. This statement does not cause any exception.

Answer: B

189. Given the code fragment:

```
public static void main(String[] args {
    List<String> lst = Arrays.asList("A", "B", "C", "D");
    Iterator<String> itr = lst.iterator();
    while(itr.hasNext()) {
        String e = itr.next();
        if (e == "C") {
            break;
        }
        else {
            continue;
            System.out.print(e);
        }
    }
}
```

Which action enables it to print Ab ?

A. Comment lines 18 to 21.

B. Comment line 20.

C. Comment line 19.

D. Comment line 16.

Answer: B

190. Given:

```
public class ComputeSum {
int x;
int y;
public int sum;
public ComputeSum (int nx, int ny) {
x = nx; y =ny;
updateSum();
}
public void setX(int nx) { x = nx; updateSum();}
public void setY(int ny) { x = ny; updateSum();}
void updateSum() { sum = x + y;}
}
```

This class needs to protect an invariant on the sum field.

Which three members must have the private access modifier to ensure that this invariant

is maintained?

A. The x field

B. The y field

C. The sum field

D. The ComputerSum ( ) constructor

E. The setX ( ) method

F. The setY ( ) method

Answer: C, E, F

191. What is the output of the following code snippet?

```
System.out.print("a");
try {
  System.out.print("b");
  throw new IllegalArgumentException();
} catch (RuntimeException e) {
  System.out.print("c");
} finally {
  System.out.print("d");

}
System.out.print("e");
```

A. abe

B. abce

C. abde

D. abcde

E. The code does not compile.

F. An uncaught exception is thrown.

Answer- D

192. Given:

```
class Overloading { int x(double d)
{ System.out.println("one"); return 0;
}
String x(double d) { System.out.println("two"); return null;
}
double x(double d) { System.out.println("three"); return 0.0;
}
public static void main(String[] args) { new Overloading().x(4.0); }
}
```

What is the result?

A. One

B. Two

C. Three

D. Compilation fails.

Answer: D

193. Given the definitions of the Bird class and the Peacock class:

```
public class Bird {
    public void fly() {
        System.out.print ("Fly.");
    }
}

public class Peacock extends Bird {
    public void dance() {
        System.out.print("Dance.");
    }
}
```

and the code fragment:

```
/*insert code snippet here */
p.fly();
p.dance();
```

and the code fragment:

```
/*insert code snippet here */
p.fly();
p.dance();
```


Which code snippet can be inserted to print Fly.Dance, ?

A. Bird p= new Peacock();

B. Bird b= new Bird(); Peacock p = (peacock) b;

C. Peacock b = new Peacock (); Bird p = (Bird) b;

D. Bird b = new Peacock (); Peacock p= (Peacock) b;

Answer: B

194. Given

```
public class Test {
    public static void main(String[] args) {
        int x = 1;
        int y = 0;
        if(x++ > ++y) {
            System.out.print("Hello ");
        } else {
            System.out.print("Welcome ");
        }
        System.out.print("Log " + x + ":" + y);
    }
}
```

What is the result?

A. Hello Log 1:0

B. Hello Log 2:1

C. Welcome Log 2:1

D. Welcome Log 1:0

Answer: C

195. Given the for loop construct:

for (expr **1** ; expr2 ; expr 3) { Statement; }

Which two statements are true?

A. This is not the only valid for loop construct; there exits another form Offor loop constructor.

B. The expression expr I is optional it initializes the loop and is evaluated once, as the loop begin.

C. When expr2 evaluates to false. the loop terminates. It is evaluated only after each

iteration through the loop.

D. The expression expr3 must be present. It is evaluated after each iteration through the loop.

Answer: B, C

196. What is the result of the following class? (Choose all that apply)

```
public class _C {
 private static int $;
 public static void main(String[] main) {
   String a_b;
   System.out.print($);
   System.out.print(a_b);
 } }
```

A. Compiler error on line 1.

B. Compiler error on line 2.

C. Compiler error on line 4.

D. Compiler error on line 5.

E. Compiler error on line 6.

F. 0null

G. nullnull

Answer: E

197. What is the output of the following program?

```
public class FeedingSchedule {
 public static void main(String[] args) {
   int x = 5, j = 0;
   OUTER: for(int i=0; i<3; )
     INNER: do {
       i++; x++;
       if(x > 10) break INNER;
       x += 4;
       j++;
      } while(j <= 2);
    System.out.println(x);
 } }
```

A. 10
B. 12
C. 13
D. 17
E. 12
F. The code will not compile because of line 4.
G. The code will not compile because of line 6

Answer: B

198. Which of the following can fill in the blank in this code to make it compile?

A. abstract
B. public
C. default
D. It will not compile with any as interfaces cannot have non abstract methods.
E. It will compile without filling the blank

Answer: C

199. Examine:

```
class E1 extends Exception { }

class E2 extends RuntimeException { }

public class App {
     public void m1() {
          System.out.println("m1.Accessed.");
          throw new E1();
     }

     public void m2 () {
          System.out.println("m2.Accessed.");
          throw new E2();
     }
     public static void main (String[] args) {
          int level =1;
          App obj = new App();
          if (level <=5 && level >= 3) {
               obj.m1();
          } else {
               obj.m2();
          }
     }
}
```

Which statement is true?

A. The program prints ml.Accessed.

B. The program fails due to Che unhandled El exception.

C. The program prints m2.Accessed .

D. The program fails to compile due to the unhandled E2 exception.

Answer: B

200. A method is declared to take three arguments. A program calls this method and passes only two arguments. What is the result?

A. Compilation fails.

B. The third argument is given the value nun.

C. The third argument is given the value void.

D. The third argument is given the value zero.

E. The third argument is given the appropriate false value for its declared type.

F. An exception occurs when the method attempts to access the third argument.

Answer: A

201.Given the code fragment int var1 = -5; int var2 = var1; int var3 = 0;

```
if (var2< O) {var3= var2++;
} else {
var3 = - -var2;
}
System.out.println(var3);
```

What is the result?

A. -6

B. -4

C. -5

D. 5

E. 4

F. Compilation fails

Answer: C

202. Given:

```
class Base {
public static void main(String[] args) { System.out.println("Base " + args[2]); }
}
public class Sub extends Base{
public static void main(String[] args) { System.out.println("Overriden " + args[1]); }
}
```

And the commands: javac Sub.java

java Sub 10 20 30 What is the result?

A. Base 30

B. Overridden 20

C. Overridden 20 Base 30

D. Base 30 Overridden 20

Answer: B

203. Given:

```
class Mid {
public int findMid(int n1, int n2) {
return (n1 + n2) / 2;
}
}
public class Calc extends Mid {
public static void main(String[] args) {
int n1 = 22, n2 = 2;
//insert code here.
System.out.print(n3);
}
}
```

Which two code fragments, when inserted at // insert code here, enable the code to compile and print 12?

A. Calc c = new Calc(); int n3 = c.findMid(n1,n2);

B. int n3 = super.findMid(n1,n3);

C. Calc c = new Mid(); int n3 = c.findMid(n1, n2);

D. Mid m1 = new Calc(); int n3 = m1.findMid(n1, n2);

E. int n3 = Calc.findMid(n1, n2);

Answer: A, D

204. Given the code fragment:

```
int a=0; a++;
System.out.println(a++); System.out.println(a);
```

What is the result?

A. 12

B. 01

C. 11

D. 22

Answer: A

205. Given the code snippet from a compiled Java source file:

```
public class MyFile
{
    public static void main (String[] args)
    {
        String arg1 = args[1];
        String arg2 = args[2];
        String arg3 = args[3];
        System.out.println("Arg is " + arg3);
    }
}
```

Which command-line arguments should you pass to the program to obtain the following output?

Arg is 2

A. java MyFile 1 3 2 2

B. java MyFile 2 2 2

C. java MyFile 1 2 2 3 4

D. java MyFile 0 1 2 3

Answer: A

206. Given the code fragment:

```
String[] strs = new String[2];
int idx = 0;
for (String s : strs) {
    strs[idx].concat(" element " + idx);
    idx++;
}
for (idx = 0; idx < strs.length; idx++) {
    System.out.println(strs[idx]);
}
```

What is the result?

A. Element 0 Element 1

B. Null element 0 Null
element 1

C. Null
Null

D. A NullPointerException is thrown at runtime.

Answer: D

207. What is the result of the following code?

```
String s1 = "Java";
String s2 = "Java";
StringBuilder sb1 = new StringBuilder();
sb1.append("Ja").append("va");
System.out.println(s1 == s2);
System.out.println(s1.equals(s2));
System.out.println(sb1.toString() == s1);
System.out.println(sb1.toString().equals(s1));
```

A. true is printed out exactly once.
B. true is printed out exactly twice.
C. true is printed out exactly three times.
D. true is printed out exactly four times.
E. The code does not compile.
Answer: C

208.Given the code fragment:

```
char colorCode = 'y';
switch (colorCode) {
  case 'r':
       int color = 100;
       break;
  case 'b':
       color = 10;
       break;
  case 'y':
       color = 1;
       break;
 }
 System.out.println(color);
```

What is the result?
A. It results in a compile time error at line 18.
B. It results in a compile time error at Line 9.
C. It prints 1
D. It results in a compile time error at lines at 12 and 15.
Answer: A

209. Given:

public class Fieldinit { char **c**;
Boolean b; float f;
void printAll() { System.out-println("c= " + c); System-out-println("c ="+ b);
System.out.println("c =" + f);
}
public static void main(String[] args) { Fieldlnit f = new Fieldlnit();
f.printAll();
}
}

What is the result?

A. c = null b = false f = 0.0F

B. c = 0 b = false f = 0.0f C. c = null b = true

f = 0.0

D. c =

b = false f = 0.0

Answer: D

210. What is the output of the following code? (Choose all that apply)

```
interface HasTail { int getTailLength(); }
abstract class Puma implements HasTail {
  protected int getTailLength() {return 4;}
}
public class Cougar extends Puma {
   public static void main(String[] args) {
     Puma puma = new Puma();

     System.out.println(puma.getTailLength());
   }

  public int getTailLength(int length) {return 2;}
 }
```

A. 2

B. 4

C. The code will not compile because of line 3.

D. The code will not compile because of line 5.

E. The code will not compile because of line 7.

F. The code will not compile because of line 11.

G. The output cannot be determined from the code provided.

Answer: C, D, E.

211. Given the code fragment int varl = -5; int var2 = varl--; int var3 - 0;

```
if (var< 0) {var 3= var2++;
} else{
var3 = --var2;
}
System.out.println(var3);
```

What is the result?

A. -6

B. -4

C. -5

D. 5

E. 4

F. Compilation fails

Answer: C

212. Which three are valid types for switch?

A. int

B. float

C. double

D. integer

E- String

F. Float

Answer: A, D, E

ONLINE RESOURCES

Practice Paper

Link : https://forms.gle/WQDRM6hpZiWnccYG9

Video Content

Link : https://www.youtube.com/playlist?list=PLzlh_31VWEFr90bIgv56c3xabjV50iFLV